W9-APE-344

God's Image of You

by
Charles Capps

Unless otherwise indicated, all Scripture quotations are taken from the *King James Version* of the Bible.

Some Scripture quotations are taken from the *Amplified Bible, New Testament.* Copyright © 1954, 1958 by the Lockman Foundation, La Habra, California.

25th Printing 2018

God's Image of You
ISBN-13: 978-0-9618975-9-8
ISBN-10: 0-9618975-9-7
FORMERLY ISBN-13: 978-0-89274-376-6
FORMERLY ISBN-10: 0-89274-376-X
Copyright © 1985 by Charles Capps
P.O. Box 69
England, Arkansas 72046

Published by CAPPS PUBLISHING
P.O. Box 69
England, AR 72046

Printed in the United States of America. All rights reserved under International Copyright Law. Contents and/or cover may not be reproduced in whole or in part in any form without the express written consent of the Publisher.

Contents

Preface

Father, I call for the supernatural wisdom of God to flow forth unhindered from these pages, to reveal the hidden things of God and to bring forth the revelation that You would desire to put in the hearts of the reader: that the image of God in the Word should come alive in them, that they may walk in a higher level of faith and understanding of Your Word.

Father, I believe You for the supernatural healing power of God to flow through Your Word to the spirit, soul, and body of every person who reads this book.

1

Seeing Yourself
as God Sees You

The business world has long ago discovered that a person will never rise above their self-image. The image you form of yourself will cause you to either succeed or fail in life.

It is not so much what or who you are that determines your fate in life, but what or who you imagine yourself to be. Your image can carry you to heights of success or plunge you into depths of defeat and despair.

It is not the things that happen to you in life that cause you to fail or succeed, *but what you believe about the things that happen to you.*

The world uses all kinds of gimmicks to raise the salesperson's self-image, for the image they have will either set them free to reach for new horizons or hold them in poverty.

One successful deal never has made anyone a success. Nor has one bad deal made anyone a failure. But sometimes that one success or failure forms an image inside that individual that governs their outlook on life and everything that happens to them.

Distorted Image

Not only is this a fact in the world system, but also in the lives of many Christians who believe God is against them because of previous failures.

They see themselves through their own critical eye. Their self-image has been distorted by condemnation of the devil. They have become deceived in their own imagination.

They think negatively. They believe negatively. They talk negatively.

Their tongue deceives their heart.

They will be crippled for life unless they find the knowledge of the truth, for it is the **knowledge of truth** that sets men free. God's Word is that truth.

When the knowledge of truth is received, then they must be a doer of that truth.

By doing what the Word says, thinking as God thinks and seeing yourself as God sees you, you allow God's Word to build your self-image.

> But be ye doers of the word, and not hearers only, deceiving your own selves.
>
> For if any be a hearer of the word, and not a doer, he is like unto a man beholding his natural face in a glass:
>
> For he beholdeth himself, and goeth his way, and straightway forgetteth what manner of man he was.
>
> But whoso looketh into the perfect law of liberty, and continueth therein, he being not a forgetful hearer, but a doer of the work, this man shall be blessed in his deed.
>
> If any man among you seem to be religious, and bridleth not his tongue, but deceiveth his own heart, this man's religion is vain.
>
> James 1:22-26

James says, "If any be a hearer of the Word, and not a doer, he is like a man beholding his natural face in a glass, who then goes his way and forgets what manner of man he was."

By getting into the Word of God, you can see yourself the way God sees you. He does not see you as you are now. He sees you as you will be after the Word does a work in you. He calls things that are not as though they were until they are.

Sons Now

Beloved, now are we the sons of God, and it doth not yet appear what we shall be: but we know that, when he shall appear, we shall be like him; for we shall see him as he is.

1 John 3:2

God says we are His sons now. *We're more than conquerors through Him that loved us.* To be more than conquerors means we can enjoy the conquest without doing all the fighting. That's more than a conqueror. You don't have to go through all the battle. Some things you must do, but some things Jesus has already done for you. You have to rest and believe in what He has already done.

God's Word says we are more than conquerors, and greater is He that is in us than He that is in the world.

Pressure Distorts Image

James describes the person who is a hearer of the Word and not a doer. He is like a man that hears who he is, but does not speak his faith and never establishes that image within himself. He walks away from the Word with joy. But when the circumstances of life slap him in the face, he says, "Oh, why does it happen to me? Why me, Lord?" He has forgotten what manner of man he was.

While he was reading God's Word and had the Word before his eyes, he thought, "Glory to God! Just let me get at the devil!" But then he walked off and forgot everything he had heard, because he did not establish that image by confessing the Word.

Have you noticed that in a meeting with others of like faith, you can believe every word of God. The Word preached gives you a glimpse of who you really are in Christ. But it takes time to establish that image within you. *If you don't get it down inside you, it will fade away.*

Unless you act immediately on God's Word and put it into motion in your life, the devil will steal it from you when you get out there and have to face the circumstances of life.

This is what happens to a lot of Christians. They come to a meeting and get so high that they can almost fly home without an airplane. But when they get home, they have to face the everyday situations of life, away from all those of like faith. It is then that they forget who they are in Christ, and Satan steals the image that was built from the Word.

The image that God puts in His Word is the image you should have of yourself. *You must have the image God has of you if you expect to fulfill the place He has designed for you in the Kingdom.*

You can't go around seeing yourself the way the devil says you are and still fulfill God's purpose for you in the Kingdom.

See yourself as God sees you. Believe what God says about you.

You must believe it longer than just while you are reading it. You must believe it when you face the circumstances of life.

Flesh Can Be Trained

But I beseech you, that I may not be bold when I am present with that confidence, wherewith I think to be bold against some, which think of us as if we walked according to the flesh.

For though we walk in the flesh, we do not war after the flesh.

2 Corinthians 10:2,3

Someone may say, "I'm afraid I'll get in the flesh."

Sometimes we've been deceived into believing that our flesh is sinful and that we always have to be beating the flesh to death. But the flesh is not necessarily sinful. Your body will do anything you train it to do.

If you receive the right images, you'll be surprised about what your body will do to fall in line with that. Your words are so important when it comes to getting your body in line with the image. Your words have everything to do with making the image a part of you.

Wrong Imagination Distorts Image

(For the weapons of our warfare are not carnal, but mighty through God to the pulling down of strong holds;)

Casting down imaginations, and every high thing that exalteth itself against the knowledge of God, bringing into captivity every thought to the obedience of Christ;

And having in a readiness to revenge all disobedience, when your obedience is fulfilled.

2 Corinthians 10:4-6

I like verse six. Paul says it's all right to revenge people who have been disobedient. Just don't do it until your obedience has been fulfilled. Now that will jerk the slack out of you.

But verse five is the one I want to zero in on: Casting down imaginations, and *every* high thing that comes against God's knowledge.

You must cast down the imaginations that put an image inside you that is contrary to what God's Word says. Get rid of it. Quit trying to see yourself as a poor sinner saved by grace.

That is one thing that has held many in bondage for years. A man thinks he's being humble by saying, "I'm just a poor, old sinner saved by grace." No, you *were* a poor, old sinner, but you were saved by grace and you became the righteousness of God in Christ Jesus. That old image should have passed away.

Developing A New Image

If any man be in Christ, he is a new creation: old things have passed away; behold, *all things* **have become new.**
2 Corinthians 5:17

All things are new in the realm of the spirit. We know the body didn't physically change in appearance. As someone stated, if you were bald-headed, getting born again didn't suddenly put hair on your head. But your spirit (or heart) has been changed.

We must realize that we're not sinners saved by grace. *We have been made the righteousness of God in Christ,* and we can be filled with the knowledge of God's will — if we'll study the Word of God.

We have the Greater One within us. We are strengthened with all might according to His glorious power, if we

believe the Word, for we are new crea-
tions in Christ.

If we were old sinners saved by grace,
then we'd keep sinning. The Bible gives
several examples of that. It talks about a
dog returning to his vomit and the hog
to his wallowing in the mire.

You can take a guy who has sinned
and clean him up. But when you turn
him loose, he'll go right back into sin if
he is not changed in his heart. He must
become a new creation. That is what has
happened many times: people have just
joined churches without getting born
again. So they go right back to their
sinning.

If I were an old sinner saved by grace,
the very next day I'd have gone right back
into sin. If grace just forgave me of my
sins, and that's all it did, it would have
to do it the next day too because I'd be
right back out there in the same thing.

But grace changed me. Grace through
faith changed me. *I became a new creation.*
I began to see myself differently. I had different desires. *I had a new spirit.*

2

Created To Have Dominion

Let's go to Genesis 1 and get an account of creation. Some of the most profound truths in the Bible are in the Book of Genesis, especially the first three chapters. If you miss that, you won't be able to understand many things in the Bible.

> **And God said, Let the earth bring forth grass, the herb yielding seed, and the fruit tree yielding fruit after his kind, whose seed is in itself, upon the earth: and it was so.**
>
> Genesis 1:11

It says the fruit tree yields fruit "after *his* kind." It didn't say, "*its* kind," although that is implied. It said, "after *his* kind." What God had in mind here is the law of double reference, referring to two different things.

It is talking about the natural tree producing after its kind. But because it said after *his* kind, whose seed is in itself;

He is also putting forth a principle here that follows in the line of the Bible from Genesis to Revelation.

Words Produce Images

Everything — whether trees, animals, man, or whatever — produce after their kind. This is what I call the law of Genesis. Everything produces after its own kind.

Words do the same thing. *Speak fear-filled words, and they will produce fear. Speak faith-filled words,* and they will produce faith. If you talk trouble and sorrow long enough, it will produce that image in you.

What you're talking is what will be produced, either faith or fear. What you continue to speak produces the image. Words produce images.

If I mentioned "airplane," you immediately would visualize an airplane. You might get an image of an airplane at an airport near you. Now if I said "twin-engine airplane," then the image would be changed. If I said "red airplane," your image would change again.

Every word I say and every description I give begins to build that image more clearly inside you. If I described my airplane in detail, you could go to the airport and find it. You would recognize it instantly, even though you've never seen it.

Someone could ask, "How could you do that? You've never seen his airplane."

"But I heard him describe it."

The reason you could recognize it instantly is because I transferred an image of that plane to you with words.

This is what God is trying to do for us: describe us in such detail, until we get that image inside us, until when He gets through describing us, *Satan can recognize us instantly as having the Greater One in us.*

> **And the earth brought forth grass, and herb yielding seed after his kind, and the tree yielding fruit, whose seed was in itself, after his kind: and God saw that it was good.**
>
> Genesis 1:12

Notice, God produced after His kind. Even when He created trees, He produced after His kind.

What kind is God? *God's kind is good and perfect.* He saw that it was good.

The most natural emphasis is that the tree produces after its kind. But the fact that He uses a personal pronoun is showing us that God produced that tree after the kind that He would produce.

That meant the tree He created to be in the Garden would have produced perfect fruit — no flaws, no rotten fruit, no soft spots, no worms, nothing that would deform the fruit — forever. It would produce perfect fruit continually.

If you took the seed from that fruit and planted it, it would produce another tree that would produce perfect fruit forever. That's God's kind. Every good and perfect gift comes from the Father of lights. (James 1:17.)

We need to get an image of the good and perfect for *that* is God's kind.

And God said, Let us make man in our image, after our likeness: and let them have dominion over the fish of the sea, and over the fowl of the air, and over the cattle, and over all the earth, and over every creeping thing that creepeth upon the earth.

**So God created man in his own
image, in the image of God created he
him; male and female created he them.**
Genesis 1:26,27

These verses are two of the most
astounding passages of Scripture in the
Bible.

But sometimes we read them and say,
"Yes, I knew God said that." But did you
really get the impact of what God said?

After He said, "Everything produces
after his kind," God created mankind
after His kind.

God said, "Let us create (or make)
man in our image, after our likeness: and
let them have dominion." This image is
the basis for man's dominion. We see it
portrayed in the Old Testament. But as we
get into the New Testament, it brings that
image out in more detail.

"Let them have dominion over the fish
of the sea." I've had people say, "You don't
really believe you have dominion over
fish. You don't really think God means
that!" No, I don't *think* it. I *know* it! *I have
fish in my freezer to prove it!*

God was not just filling the pages of the Bible when He said that.

Aligning Your Image With God's Image of You

Several years ago the Lord said to me, "You need to go back and read the Bible like you never heard it before. Forget everything religious you've ever heard about it, and read it like you never heard it before."

So I started in Genesis, chapter 1. I got to verse 26 and said, "Thank God, I have dominion over the fish of the sea. If I have dominion over the fish of the sea, I have dominion over the bass of the lake."

I took that scripture, along with Psalm 1:3 — *Whatsoever he doeth shall prosper* — and I caught more bass than ever before.

Someone asked one day, "What did you catch that string of bass on?" I said, "Genesis 1:28 and Psalm 1:3." I have dominion over the fish of the sea, and whatever I do will prosper.

This is establishing mankind's dominion. That includes ladies as well. There's no male nor female in Christ.

I have this image of dominion because of continually teaching on the subject. That image has become more perfected as a result of continuing to speak and hear God's image of me.

Because of that, the time span from when I speak until the manifestation comes is getting shorter. The more developed you get in either fear or faith, the quicker the manifestation will come.

That's why some things happen quickly to people when they just say a few bad things. Then they say, "I don't know why things happen so quickly when I say something bad. But when I say something good, I have to say it six months before it ever comes to pass." *It's because they are more developed in the negative than in the positive.*

Your imagination creates pictures inside you. You have to cast down imaginations that are not in line with God's Word. When you imagine things, you begin to talk that way. As you talk that way, that image in you is perfected, whether it's on the positive side or the negative side.

When God said mankind has dominion *over all the earth,* I believe He meant what He said. **All** the earth. So in the past several years, I've talked to pieces of property I wanted to sell. I've picked up handfuls of dirt and said, "I have dominion over you. I'm telling you that somebody is impressed with you. They like you. You are sold, in the name of Jesus."

Some may think I am an absolute nut. I might be in their eyes, but I am the nut who sold the houses and the property.

Do you think a house would obey you? Jesus said it would. He said a tree would, and He proved it. (Mark 11:20,21.)

Dominion over all the earth. God gave mankind dominion over everything that creeps on the earth. Don't let a creep get you all upset. You have dominion over creeps. You have dominion over everything that *creepeth* on the earth!

3

In the Image of God

Let's look again at Genesis 1:27,28.

So God created man in his own image, in the image of God created he him; male and female created he them.

And God blessed them, and God said unto them, Be fruitful, and multiply, and replenish the earth, and subdue it: and have dominion over the fish of the sea, and over the fowl of the air, and over every living thing that moveth upon the earth.

What you see here is the image that was inside God before He created man.

Let us create man in our image. Who is *us*? The Father, the Son, and the Holy Spirit.

Man is such an exact duplication of God that he is a three-fold being: spirit, soul, and body. He is a spirit, he has a soul, and he lives in a body. Each part relates to the Father, the Son, and the Holy Ghost.

The physical body relates to Jesus, — the physical manifestation of God on the earth.

The spirit of man relates to God, Who is a spirit.

The soulish realm of man, composed of his will, mind, and emotions, relates to the Holy Spirit, Who is our guide. Jesus said, **"When He is come, He will teach you all things and guide you into all truth."** (John 16:13.) The soul — will, mind, and emotions — of man makes him do what he does.

> **And God blessed the seventh day, and sanctified it: because that in it he had rested from all his work which God created and made.**
>
> Genesis 2:3

Notice God *created* some and *made* others. The earth was created. Then verse 7 says, **The Lord God formed man of the dust of the ground.** He didn't create man; He *formed* man. The footnote says He *molded* him out of the dust of the ground.

God created the earth. Then He took the dirt or dust that was already created and formed man's body.

That's like somebody chopping down a tree, and building a house. That person didn't create the house. The tree already existed. He just moved it, changed its form, and made it into a house.

The Life of God Imparted

God *formed man's body* out of the dust of the ground. The rest of that verse tells how the creation came into being. **God breathed into his nostrils the breath of life; and man became a living soul.** God breathed into man's nostrils the spirit of life. Man is a living spirit being with a physical body.

God had made man's body with arms, legs, heart, lungs, eyes, everything in place — a perfect specimen of God's image of man. But *that man was just a dead piece of clay until God breathed into him the spirit of life* — **It was the life of God.**

God breathed into Adam the life that was inside Himself; and *Adam became an exact duplication of God's kind.*

Remember the law of Genesis. God does not produce after somebody else's kind. He always produces after His kind.

He said, "Let us make man in *our* image, after *our* likeness."

That's hard to receive until you understand what God's kind is. Jesus said, **God is a spirit: and they that worship him must worship him in spirit and in truth.**

Some people have an image of God being 400 feet tall with arms as big as a building. But why would God make man a different size than He is? I'm convinced He made man just like Himself.

Isaiah says God measured out the heavens by the span of His hand. (Is. 40:12.) The footnote there says that is 9½ inches. That's about the span of a normal hand from the thumb to the little finger. If God did it with His hand, in His 9½ inches, it seems to me He's talking about the same image.

God doesn't have a physical body; but He has a spiritual body, and He can take a physical form.

First John 4:12 says no man has ever seen God at any time. It's talking about seeing God in all of His splendor, power, and glory. No man could see God and live.

The idea that nobody has ever seen God is wrong. **God appeared in bodily form to many in the Bible.**

Abraham talked face to face with God. He saw Him coming one day with two other men. It was God Himself. He walked right up to Abraham and talked to him.

Moses saw Him. Isaac saw Him. God didn't look like a big mountain when they saw Him. He looked like a man.

God has created man in His image, and in His likeness. **God breathed into his nostrils the breath of life, and man became a living soul.**

But then man fell. He made the wrong choice in the Garden. He became subordinate to Satan.

When Satan came into the Garden to deceive Eve, he had to borrow a body from a serpent before he could do anything.

The earthly body is a vehicle of authority. That is why God through the Holy Ghost wants to inhabit your body.

Your body gives authority of expression.

This is also why the devil wants to get inside people. He is limited in what he can do without a body through which to manifest himself. The devil and evil spirits can do very little unless they have a body.

Satan is illegal on the earth. He's a created being. He has no authority here because he wasn't born here. Mankind had rightful dominion of the whole earth.

Though Adam had it good, it only took him a short time to foul things up. But Jesus came and restored dominion.

You're created in the image of God, in His likeness. Jesus has restored you to your rightful order.

Under His Feet

For unto the angels hath he not put in subjection the world to come, whereof we speak.

But one in a certain place testified, saying, What is man, that thou art mindful of him? or the son of man, that thou visitest him?

Thou madest him a little lower than the angels; thou crownedst him with

**glory and honour, and didst set him over
the works of thy hands:**

**Thou hast put all things in subjection
under his feet**.

Hebrews 2:5-8

God has not put the world to come
in subjection to the angels. He has put it
in subjection to men.

Verse 6 is referring not only to man,
but also to the Son of Man. It's referring
to man and the Son of Man because Jesus
came to the earth as a man, and He was
anointed with the Holy Ghost to destroy
the works of the devil. *His authority came
from the fact that He was a man, born on the
earth.*

**Thou hast put all things in subjection
under his feet.** "All things." Think about
it. God gave man dominion over
everything that moves upon this earth or
swims in the sea. But we must know how
to appropriate that authority and exercise
that dominion.

**Even if you know how, unless you see
yourself as God sees you, you won't act
on it.** You have to believe you have the

authority to do it, and then see yourself through the eyes of God.

Man's Role in God's Kingdom

Thou hast put all things in subjection under his feet. For in that he put all in subjection under him, he left nothing that is not put under him. But now we see not yet all things put under him. (v. 8.)

This verse proves it's not only talking about Jesus, but also about man.

But now we see not yet all things put under him (man). **But we see Jesus who was made a little lower than the angels.** Everything is now put under the feet of Jesus.

This points out that we should see ourselves as Jesus was. We should walk in the same authority, power, and dominion that Jesus exercised when He walked this earth.

God's will and purpose for this earth is that it be here like it is in heaven. It has to be the will of God because Jesus told His disciples to pray that it would be that way. (Matt. 6:10.)

It's God's will that His creation (mankind) have dominion over this earth and subdue it. Adam was created to be ruler over the earth. *God did not intend for man to be bowled over by the circumstances of life,* always in trouble and just fighting to survive.

Actually, man is supposed to be god over the earth. God gave him dominion over it. He said, "There it is, Adam. It's yours. You can do what you want with it. But don't eat of the tree of the knowledge of blessing and calamity, for the day that you eat you will surely die."

But Adam did eat of that tree.

Why didn't God stop him?

It wasn't God's responsibility. Adam was ruler over the earth. He could do what he wanted with it. So he sold the earth lease to Satan, and Satan became the god of the world. **. . .the god of this world has blinded the minds of them that believe not** (2 Cor. 4:4).

Where did Satan get the title of being god of the world? He got it from Adam. Satan is god of the world system, not god over the believer.

Keeping the Right Perspective

There is a fine line here between truth and error. I realize we're walking a tightrope. We don't want to get off into error in anything. There is some teaching going around that man is God. Adam was god over earth, but you spell it with a little "g." He was certainly under God, but the earth was his responsibility.

We're created in the image of God. We were to be god (ruler) over the earth. **But let's keep it in the right perspective.** That is what got the devil into trouble: thinking he was God.

We're not God, and we're never going to be God. **We are sons of God,** joint-heirs with Jesus. We were created to be gods over the earth, but remember to spell it with a little "g."

In John 10:30-33, Jesus said:

> I and my Father are one.
>
> Then the Jews took up stones again to stone him.
>
> Jesus answered them, Many good works have I showed you from my Father; for which of those works do ye stone me?

The Jews answered him, saying, For a good work we stone thee not; but for blasphemy; *and because that thou, being a man, makest thyself God.*

Religious people always get disturbed when you even imply that you are righteous. Some churches that call themselves "Full Gospel" will not allow a certain music tape to be played in their services, because one verse says, "I am the righteousness of God in Christ." They don't want anyone singing about being the righteousness of God in Christ. They're still *poor old sinners saved by grace.*

Religious people will get upset over what Jesus said about us, and what Paul said about us, even what God said about us. *Religious spirits don't want you seeing yourself through the eyes of God.*

This is where the dividing line is in these last days between people who see themselves the way God sees them, and people who see themselves the way religion sees them.

Religion sees you as a poor old sinner saved by grace, living on "barely-get-along street," never able to have anything in this life. If you're lucky, you'll make it to heaven where God will build you a cabin in the corner of gloryland. *We must be delivered from such thinking if we are to fulfill God's plan for our lives.*

Many of these people are right in their hearts, but wrong in their heads. Their minds are made up and they don't want to be confused with the facts.

In John 10:34-36, Jesus is about to be stoned, and He says:

Is it not written in your law, I said, Ye are gods?

If he called them gods, unto whom the word of God came, and the scripture cannot be broken;

Say ye of him, whom the Father hath sanctified, and sent into the world, Thou blasphemest; because I said, I am the Son of God?

Notice He just took them back to their own law to prove His point. He said, "Don't you know that it's written in your scroll where God said, Ye are gods, to whom the Word of God came?"

Sometimes people say, "Well, I don't know about being in the image of God and in His likeness. Is there anyone else who believed it that way?"

Jesus believed it that way.

He preached them a sermon from Psalm 82.

God standeth in the congregation of the mighty; he judgeth among the gods.
Psalm 82:1

God stands in the congregation of the mighty. The word translated *mighty,* is *elohim.* It is the same word translated *gods* at the end of the verse.

It literally reads this way, "Elohim standeth in the congregation of elohim, and judgeth among the elohim." God said it, and Jesus verified it being in their law.

Perfect in Christ

The Body of Christ will fulfill God's purpose in the earth when they understand this truth and begin to act as though it were true.

I'm not talking about becoming a kooky Christian. Stay within the bounds and limits of the Scriptures, but take your

image to the full height of what God says
you are.

**You are not God. You will never be
God. But you are to be god over the circumstances and situations of this earth
through the power of God, through the
anointing of God, through Christ being
in you in the person of the Holy Ghost.**
The fullness of the Godhead dwells in the
Body of Christ. This is what God is trying to get over to us.

Jesus said in John 14:23, **"If you will
keep *My* words, we** (the Father, Son, and
Holy Ghost) **will come unto you and
make our abode with you."** But so many
people keep casting out the words. The
Word of God builds an image of what you
are and who you are in Christ.

When I'm talking about who we are,
I'm talking about being in Christ. I'm not
righteous within myself. But I'm not in
myself. Thank God! I'm in Jesus, and
Jesus is in me.

These are the words of Jesus as He
prayed in John 17: **I in them, and thou
in me, that they may be made perfect in**

one (v. 23). *Perfect.* Did you know that Christians can be perfect today? *We can* be perfect *in Christ.*

When you are in Christ, God does not see you for what you actually are; He sees you through what Jesus did to make you perfect.

When God looks at you in Christ, He does not see your impurities; He sees you in Christ.

Then it is your responsibility to confess your sin when you make a mistake. According to 1 John 1:9, it cleanses you from all unrighteousness. You are forgiven, and God sees you through Christ as being pure.

That is the way we are perfect today. I don't mean to infer that we never make any mistakes. Christians are not *perfect* in that sense. We're just *forgiven.* But God sees you perfect. He sees you in the image that He created you.

4

Man and the Angels

Look again at Psalm 82, verse 1:

God standeth in the congregation of the mighty; he judgeth among the gods.

Someone may say, "I know what that means. It means the Father, the Son, and the Holy Ghost."

That sounds good until you read the second verse.

How long will ye judge unjustly, and accept the persons of the wicked? Selah.

Are you going to accuse God, the Holy Ghost, or Jesus of judging unjustly? No. This is talking about men.

Defend the poor and fatherless: do justice to the afflicted and needy.

Deliver the poor and needy: rid them out of the hand of the wicked.

They know not, neither will they understand; they walk on in darkness:

all the foundations of the earth are out of course.

I have said, Ye are gods; and all of you are children of the most High.

But ye shall die like men, and fall like one of the princes.

Arise, O God, judge the earth: for thou shalt inherit all nations.

Psalm 82:3-8

Now, let's look at Psalm 8.

When I consider thy heavens, the work of thy fingers, the moon and the stars, which thou hast ordained;

What is man, that thou art mindful of him? and the son of man, that thou visitest him?

For thou hast made him a little lower than the angels, and hast crowned him with glory and honour.

Thou madest him to have dominion over the works of thy hands; thou hast put all things under his feet.

Psalm 8:3-6

This is what the writer of Hebrews is referring to when he says, *What is man?* (Heb. 2:6). He's quoting Psalm 8.

Hebrews 2:7 in the *King James Version* says, **Thou madest him** (man) **a little**

lower than the angels. This is one of the problems in seeing yourself the way God sees you. There must be a clear understanding of this scripture. Man was not created lower than the angels. **He was created lower than** *Elohim.* In verse 7 the Greek word used did mean *angels,* but it was translated from Psalm 8:5.

This word in the Hebrew translated *angels* is the same word used in Psalm 82: *Elohim.* It doesn't mean angels at all. It is plural for God.

"Thou hast made him a little lower than gods." Man was created in God's image, in His likeness, but he was made lower than God Himself. However, he was to be god, or ruler, over the earth.

In the Garden it was Adam, not angels, who was given authority and dominion over the earth. *Man then fell below the angels.* The world to come will be put in subjection to men. Once again, it will be mankind, not angels, who will rule during the Millennium.

In the Garden Adam had the right to make a choice. God told him not to eat of the fruit of the tree of the knowledge of good and evil. Adam not only had a choice, he had *the right* to make that choice. The way he chose was the way it would be. In so many words, God said, "There it is, Adam. It's up to you."

Angels are created beings. Lucifer was a created being, an anointed cherub. He had the ability to choose, but he did not have the right to do so.

Angels do not have the right of choice. They were designed of God for specific purposes. They are not to go out of the limitation of those purposes. Once they do, it's curtains for them. There is no salvation for fallen angels.

The restitution of all things does not include fallen angels, nor the devil. Their doom is sealed.

You might ask, "Why would God redeem man and not redeem the angels?" Because angels did not have the right of choice. They had the ability to choose, but not the right.

Adam had the right of choice. God gave him the right to choose, and he made the wrong choice. Then God set about to redeem mankind. But man was not created lower than angels, he was created on a higher order in that He had the ability and right to choose. He was created a little lower than *Elohim*.

5

Speaking the Image

Let's look at verses 1 and 2 of Psalm 8:

O Lord our Lord, how excellent is thy name in all the earth! who hast set thy glory above the heavens.

Out of the mouth of babes and sucklings hast thou ordained strength because of thine enemies, that thou mightest still the enemy and the avenger.

God has ordained strength to come out of the mouths of babes — little ones! Strength will come out of their mouths "...because of thine enemies."

In other words God is saying, "My power will flow through those who are My children. Strength will come out of their mouths because of the enemy." Because the enemy had power, the enemy was lording it over them. **But strength is going to come out of their mouths.** God has ordained it.

The creative power of God will work for you as you speak it. Your words based upon the authority of God's Word. This has been ordained that we might still the enemy and the avenger with words — specifically, the Word of God, for it is the power of God.

Let's go back to the creation of the earth. How did God do it? With words. He had an image inside of Him of an earth that was dry and filled with light. But at that moment the earth was covered with water and darkness was upon the face of the deep. The Spirit of God was moving over the face of the water, *but nothing changed until God spoke the image that was inside Him.*

Even though God had the image inside Him and the Spirit of God was there to cause it to come to pass, it had to be released out of His mouth before any changes could take place.

Today you can have an image inside you. You may even have the Word of God for it. The Spirit of God may be moving concerning the very thing you have an image of, but until you release that image through faith-filled words, very little will happen to bring that into being.

You must speak that image. You must give voice to it. You give substance to that image by releasing your faith in words.

You can see what God did. He took the image that was inside Him and spoke it out. God created us in His image and likeness. Everything produces after its kind.

Why would God say everything produces after its kind, then create man after some other kind? **It would have been foolish for Him to change His own rules in the creation of man.**

Genesis 1 reads like it does so you will know how God created. "And God said...And God said...And God said...." Ten times in Genesis 1 you find that phrase. It would have been sufficient to have "And God said" only once, then list all the things God said, except that God was trying to get over to us what caused creation — **words.**

Remember Psalm 8:2 tells us that out of the mouth of babes and sucklings He has ordained strength, *that they might still the avenger.*

It's illegal for God to come to earth and destroy the work of the devil with His divine Godhead powers. He delivered the authority of this earth to man and has never taken it back. It's still in the hands of man. Adam turned it over to Satan, but Jesus took it from the devil and gave it back to the believer before He ascended to heaven.

He said, **All power is given unto me in heaven and in earth. Go ye therefore....** (Matt. 28:18,19). He delivered that authority back to man.*

Mankind:
A Channel for God's Power

God has to channel that authority through His children on the earth. He says, "I've ordained it to work this way. Out of their mouths I have ordained strength to still the avenger."

---

*More complete teaching on this subject is available in Charles Capps' book, *Your Spiritual Authority.* Available at your local bookstore.

God took the image that was inside of Him and spoke it out. When you get an image of how God sees you, begin to voice it. As you continue to speak in line with His Word, you will be perfecting that image.

God used His words to bring the image into manifestation. He filled His words with the spiritual force of faith, then used those words as containers to carry His faith into the vast nothingness to give substance to that image.

Even though He was looking at darkness, God conveyed an image of light. He took His words and framed the world. The Word is what created the world. (Heb. 11:3.)

The image inside you is *produced* by words and also *released* in words. God's Word causes faith to come, then faith-filled words perfect the image. Words release the image and give substance to it. It is a complete cycle.

When you speak what you believe, you believe what you speak. The more you believe it, the more you say it. The more you say it, the more you believe it. That image is perfected in you. The more it comes and goes through that cycle, the stronger it becomes in you.

That's why it is so important to confess God's Word: say what God says about you instead of what the devil says. If you quote what the devil says, it will create the image of what he wants to happen inside you. Remember fear-filled words produce fear. Faith-filled words produce faith.

God created man in His image and likeness with words. **With your words, you can still the avenger, stop the enemy's words, and subdue them with God's Word.**

For whatever you bind on earth is bound in heaven. Whatever you loose on earth is loosed in heaven. (Matt. 16:19.)

You have authority to bind off the earth what is bound out of heaven. You have authority to loose on earth what is loosed in heaven.

Ask yourself: "How is it in heaven? Is there sickness, disease, poverty?" No.

Then you have authority to bind it here on earth. You can't bind it off the whole earth, but *you can bind it off the part you're walking on.* Get that image inside you. Realize you have dominion over the part of the earth you're walking on.

God spoke what He wanted, not what He didn't want. That faith force was transported by words, and it continued through the Bible from Genesis to Revelation. **Any image that is perfected within you will flow out of your mouth.**

God's Word and Your Faith at Work

When you first start confessing God's Word about a situation in your life, you are causing faith to come. As you continue to speak God's Word, you destroy the old image and perfect a new image inside you.

When you're quoting God's Word over a situation, but are looking at the very opposite, then you have to cast down the image you are seeing with your physical eye. You bring it down, because the weapons of your warfare are not carnal;

they are spiritual forces flowing from within you.

When you look at apparent defeat or lack and say, "My God has met my need according to His riches in glory," you are casting down imaginations.

Your imagination is saying, "You're lying. Your need is not met."

But you start saying it like God said it. "Because I have given, it's given unto me." *When you first say it, you may not believe it.* You may say, "I know it's really not true in my situation, but I'm saying it because the Bible said it. I know it will come to pass."

As you confess that God has met your needs, you have to cast down imaginations of lack. The best way to do that is by saying what God has said in His Word. That will cause faith to come and the image to be changed.

It may take six months to change that "lack" image inside you, but it will bow to the Word of God.

It may take six months to change that "nothing better" image inside you, like the woman with the issue of blood. She had spent all she had on physicians and was nothing better. **She had a "grow worse" image, but she changed that with her words.** You can do the same.

Though the first stages of confession may not seem to do anything, they are changing an image and causing faith to come. Faith comes by hearing God's Word. Keep hearing yourself speak God's Word, and faith will come.

When that image in you is changed and faith has come, your words are not just confessions. Your words are not just changing images; they become creative power. When you speak, you will speak to affect things. Your words will change the order of things.

Then you will realize this really does work. You will say, "I do have dominion over circumstances." Then the devil has a problem. He can't prevail against the Word of God.

6

Doers of the Word Are Winners in Life

But be ye doers of the word, and not hearers only, deceiving your own selves.
James 1:22

If you are not a doer of the Word — if you don't bridle your tongue — you will deceive your heart. You will sow the wrong words, and that's the kind of harvest you will reap. The seed you sow will produce after its kind.

Many people wonder why things turn out the way they do. It is because their tongue deceived their heart, and the heart brings forth fruit of itself.

Jesus made this statement in Matthew 12: "A good man out of the good deposit, or good treasure, of his heart bringeth forth good things." Who brings it forth? *The good man.* From where? Out of the good deposit of his heart.

What you deposit in your heart is what will come forth. Out of the abundance of the heart, the mouth speaks. What's abundantly in your heart will get in your mouth. What's abundantly in your mouth will get in your heart.

You get it in your heart by saying it with your mouth. Paul tells us this in Romans 10: "The righteousness which is of faith would say this: The word is nigh thee, even in thy mouth, and in thy heart." It gets in your mouth first, then it gets in your heart.

Jesus made a confirmation of this in Luke 17:5,6. When the apostles asked Him to increase their faith, He said, **If ye had faith as a grain of mustard seed, ye might say unto this sycamine tree, Be thou plucked up by the root, and be thou planted in the sea; and it should obey you.**

He didn't say a thing about giving them more faith. He was telling them how faith should be planted. You plant it by saying it.

Isn't it amazing how the teachings throughout the Scriptures coincide and come together with the same truth? Jesus said you plant the Word, the seed of faith, by saying it.

If you had faith as a seed, you would say....

But so many people don't have faith as a seed. They say, "I wouldn't say that. It might not happen." It probably won't, because they don't have faith as a seed.

You have to plant a seed if you expect to reap a harvest. Even so, you have to release your faith, and you have to do it in words.

Planting Produces Image of Harvest

And he said, So is the kingdom of God, as if a man should cast seed into the ground;

And should sleep, and rise night and day, and the seed should spring and grow up, he knoweth not how.

For the earth bringeth forth fruit of herself; first the blade, then the ear, after that the full corn in the ear.

**But when the fruit is brought forth,
immediately he putteth in the sickle,
because the harvest is come.**

Mark 4:26-29

The earth brings forth fruit of herself.
The heart (spirit) of man will bring forth
the fruit. It will lead you to the very thing
you're saying. It will lead you to the infor-
mation. It will lead you to the situation.

It may lead you across five states to
cause what you're saying to come to pass
— good, bad, or indifferent.

A good man out of the good treasure
of his heart brings forth good things. An
evil man out of the evil treasure brings
forth evil things. I don't believe Jesus was
necessarily talking about the wicked man,
for a lot of Christians have evil things in
their heart.

James says that if you seem to be
religious and don't bridle your tongue,
you deceive your own heart, your religion
is in vain. What you believe is in vain
unless you get your mouth in line with it.

God's Word Reflects
What and Who You Are

**For if any be a hearer of the word, and
not a doer, he is like unto a man
beholding his natural face in a glass**.

James 1:23

The glass James is talking about is the Word of God. The Bible refers several times to the Word as a glass or mirror. He's calling the glass the Word of God. The natural face could be the face you inherited.

You look into this Word and see what God said about you. You say, "Look what I've inherited." You see that you are a joint-heir with Jesus. You think, "Glory to God!"

Then you go out and face the circumstances of life, forgetting what manner of man you were **unless** you act on what the Word of God says.

Notice what God has said concerning you as a believer. Let's look at what Paul prayed. It's a prayer anointed by the Holy Spirit.

**Wherefore I also, after I heard of your
faith in the Lord Jesus, and love unto all
the saints,**

Cease not to give thanks for you, making mention of you in my prayers;

That the God of our Lord Jesus Christ, the Father of glory, may give unto you the spirit of wisdom and revelation in the knowledge of him:

The eyes of your understanding being enlightened; that ye may know what is the hope of his calling, and what the riches of the glory of his inheritance in the saints,

(God considers us His inheritance.)

And what is the exceeding greatness of his power to us-ward who believe, according to the working of his mighty power.

Which he wrought in Christ, when he raised him from the dead, and set him at his own right hand in the heavenly places,

Far above all principality, and power, and might, and dominion, and every name that is named, not only in this world, but also in that which is to come:

And hath put all things under his feet, and gave him to be the head over all things to the church,

Which is his body, the fulness of him that filleth all in all.

Ephesians 1:15-23

This would be great if Paul had just stopped there, but he didn't. He went on to say:

And you hath he quickened, who were dead in trespasses and sins;

Wherein in time past ye walked according to the course of this world, according to the prince of the power of the air, the spirit that now worketh in the children of disobedience:

Even when we were dead in sins, hath quickened us together with Christ, (by grace ye are saved;).

Ephesians 2:1,2,5

One With Him

Here the writer tells us by inspiration of God that God sees us quickened together with Christ. He doesn't see the Body and the Head separated.

This is one of the great truths of the Scriptures. God the Father, the Son, and the Holy Ghost are in you, as Jesus stated in John 14:23 — *If any man loves Me, he will keep My words, and My Father will love him and we will come unto him and make our abode with him.*

Loving God and keeping His Word creates the lifestyle of God within you. And God will inhabit you in the fullness of the Godhead.

Once that happens, you can hardly tell where you quit and the Holy Ghost begins, or where God quits and Jesus begins. You can't separate it. All become one. This is the mystery Jesus spoke of when He said, "I in them, and Thou in me, that they may be perfect in one."

> **Even when we were dead in sins, hath quickened us together with Christ . . .**
>
> **And hath raised us up together, and made us sit together in heavenly places in Christ Jesus.**
>
> Ephesians 2:5,6

We were crucified with Christ. As far as God is concerned, every person died when Christ died, because the penalty for sin had to be paid and all have sinned.

Paul said, "I thus judge, *if Christ died for all, then are all dead.*" As far as God is concerned, every person has already died. Not only that, *He sees you quickened together with Christ and raised up together with Him.*

That in the ages to come he might shew the exceeding riches of his grace in his kindness toward us through Christ Jesus.

For by grace are ye saved through faith; and that not of yourselves; it is the gift of God:

Not of works, lest any man should boast.

Ephesians 2:7-9

It is the grace that is the gift of God. He's not referring to faith as being the gift of God. We've considered that to be true for so long. But look at chapter three of Ephesians:

Whereof I was made a minister, according to the gift of the grace of God given unto me by the effectual working of his power.

Unto me, who am less than the least of all saints, is this grace given, that I should preach among the Gentiles the unsearchable riches of Christ.

Ephesians 3:7,8

He's talking about the grace that is given. I think we've missed it by saying Ephesians 2:8 is referring to faith being the gift of God. There is a gift of faith, but it is one of the nine gifts of the Spirit. He's not referring to the gift of faith here. He's referring to the gift of grace.

God has raised us up together and made us sit together in heavenly places.

We're not physically in heaven right now, and Jesus is not physically here on earth. Yet Jesus has ascended to the Father and is seated at the right hand of the Father. He is making intercession for us.

7

Above Principalities and Powers

Jesus has been raised far above all principality, power, might, and dominion. He is seated above all powers, and we have been raised up together and made to sit with Him, in spiritual likeness and authority.

He's not here physically except through the Church, as His Body. *The only physical body Jesus has on the earth today is the Church — the Body of Christ.*

If God is going to heal the sick, raise the dead, and cast out demons, He will do it through you and me as the Body of Christ anointed with the Holy Ghost. Your body gives you authority on this planet.

Jesus is the Head of the Church, and we are the Body. He is seated at the right hand of the Father until His enemies are made His footstool. *God sees us as the physical Body of Christ,* the one that will do the work in the earth until Jesus descends from the right hand of the Father. But *that won't happen until His enemies are under His feet.*

If you want to accelerate Jesus' return to earth, then start putting the devil under your feet.

As far as God is concerned, He sees us exalted and seated at His right hand in spiritual power and authority, with the Head (Jesus). He sees Jesus here on earth in every one of us, **making up the actual Body of Christ upon this earth.**

Jesus has no less power, no less glory, no less authority than He had when He walked the shores of Galilee. God sees us that way — with power, authority, and His anointing within us.

For we are his workmanship, created in Christ Jesus unto good works, which God hath before ordained that we should walk in them.

Ephesians 2:10

God sees us as His workmanship. He doesn't create unworthy workmanship, and we are His workmanship. We are created in His likeness.

> **For through him we both have access by one Spirit unto the Father.**
>
> **Now therefore ye are no more strangers and foreigners, but fellowcitizens with the saints, and of the household of God.**
>
> Ephesians 2:18,19

We're fellowcitizens with the saints in heaven. As far as God is concerned, we're already there, seated with Him in power and authority. God doesn't see us as a stranger or a pilgrim, but as a fellowcitizen and a member of His household.

One Family

> **For this cause I bow my knees unto the Father of our Lord Jesus Christ,**
>
> **Of whom the whole family in heaven and earth is named.**
>
> Ephesians 3:14,15

Notice Paul didn't say there was one family on earth and one family in heaven. He said the *whole family in heaven and in earth*. God sees us all as one family — now.

Citizens in Heaven

For our conversation is in heaven; from whence also we look for the Saviour, the Lord Jesus Christ.

Philippians 3:20

That word *conversation* does not mean our speech. The Greek meaning is citizenship. Paul says our *citizenship is in heaven.*

Now you can understand what Jesus meant in John 17:11 when He stood before the disciples and prayed, "I'm no more in this world." He was calling those things that be not as though they were. He was also calling His citizenship in heaven. Thank God, our citizenship is not of this world.

8

God's Hope of Glory

Even the mystery which hath been hid from ages and from generations, but now is made manifest to his saints:

To whom God would make known what is the riches of the glory of this mystery among the Gentiles; which is Christ in you, the hope of glory.

Colossians 1:26,27

Christ in you is the hope of glory. This is the mystery that's been hid from ages and from generations and is now manifest to the saints. God's hope of glory is that *Christ live in you in this earth, that the Body of Christ would be the fullness of Him that filleth all in all, filled with God Himself.* This is the way God sees you if you are born again.

Renewed in Knowledge After His Image

Lie not one to another, seeing that ye have put off the old man with his deeds;

71

> **And have put on the new man, which is renewed in knowledge after the image of him that created him.**
>
> Colossians 3:9,10

Having His Wisdom

By being born again, you have put off the old man and have put on the new man which is renewed after the image of God.

When we put off the old man and put on the new man, we're in a position to be renewed in the knowledge after the image of Him that created him. *God sees you in His image and likeness. He sees you having His wisdom.*

A New Creature — Ambassador

> **Therefore if any man be in Christ, he is a new creature: old things are passed away; behold, all things are become new.**
>
> **And all things are of God, who hath reconciled us to himself by Jesus Christ, and hath given to us the ministry of reconciliation...**
>
> **Now then we are ambassadors for Christ, as though God did beseech you by us: we pray you in Christ's stead, be ye reconciled to God.**

For he hath made him to be sin for
us, who knew no sin; that we might be
made the righteousness of God in him.
2 Corinthians 5:17-21

Righteousness of God

God does not see you the way you
were. He sees you as a new creation. If
you've been born again, the Bible says
you are the *righteousness of God in Christ*.
For you to voice anything else or act any
other way is a slap in the face of Jesus.
It would be like saying, "Jesus, Your
righteousness is not good enough for
me." There are many that are in the same
position as Paul described in Romans
10:2,3.

For I bear them record that they have
a zeal of God, but not according to
knowledge.

For they being ignorant of God's
righteousness, and going about to
establish their own righteousness, have
not submitted themselves unto the
righteousness of God.

Romans 10:2,3

God sees you through the
righteousness of Jesus, not through your
weakness or lack. He sees you through

Christ Jesus, and He sees you *perfect in Christ.*

Strive For Perfection

You should strive for perfection. If you make a mistake, confess your sins and allow Jesus to bring you up to what God's Word says you are: the righteousness of God. God will see you as perfect in Christ.

Awake To Righteousness and Sin Not

Do as Paul said: *Awake to righteousness and sin not.* When you awake to the fact that you are the righteousness of God, (not a poor unworthy sinner), *you'll lose the desire to sin.*

God's Temple

Your body is the temple of the Holy Ghost. God sees your body as His temple, His house to dwell in. You create the lifestyle of God by thinking, speaking, and acting as God would in your situations. Then you can't keep God the Father, the Son, and the Holy Ghost from living big inside you. He delights to dwell in the temple that was prepared for Him.

Ambassador Lifestyle

Have you ever considered that you are an ambassador for Christ? I heard Marte Tilton say this:

"When our country sends ambassadors to foreign nations, they don't live like the people in that country. They live the same lifestyle as in the country of their citizenship. They live in that embassy just as they would in America. They eat the best and drive the best." And how true it is today. An ambassador has his whole nation behind him. An ambassador lives in a controlled environment in that foreign country, just as if he were here in the United States. Should it be any different for ambassadors of Christ?

This is what Paul was trying to get over to us. While we're here, we ought to live here like we were already in heaven.

How does God feel about us? God's Word calls us citizens of heaven.

To know how you should be living on this earth, you'll have to find out how it is in heaven. There's no poverty or lack, no sickness, no disease. Heaven is a healthy place.

Jesus is the Head of the Body, and He's coming after a Body that fits the Head (Jesus), a Body in unity with the Head, and that looks like Him. If you want to know what He looks like, the Word says all things are under His feet. (Heb. 2:8.)

Fullness of Christ

And he gave some, apostles; and some, prophets; and some, evangelists; and some, pastors and teachers;

For the perfecting of the saints, for the work of the ministry, for the edifying of the body of Christ:

Till we all come in the unity of the faith, and of the knowledge of the Son of God, unto a perfect man, unto the measure of the stature of the fulness of Christ.

Ephesians 4:11-13

Notice, He didn't mention *the unity of the doctrine.* He said *the unity of faith.* Verse 13 in *The Ampilifed Bible* puts it all in perspective:

[That it might develop] until we all attain oneness in the faith and in the comprehension of the full and accurate knowledge of the Son of God; that [we might arrive] at really mature manhood — the completeness of personality which is nothing less than the standard height of Christ's own perfection — the measure of the stature of the fullness of the Christ, and the completeness found in Him.

God sees you this way. Should you see or be any less?

For a complete list of CDs, DVDs, and books
by Capps Ministries, write:

Capps Ministries
P.O. Box 69, England, Arkansas 72046

Toll Free Order Line (24 hours)
1-877-396-9400

E-Books
& MP3's
Available

www.cappsministries.com
Visit us online for:

Radio Broadcasts in Your Area
Concepts of Faith Television Broadcast listings:
Local Stations, **Daystar**, & **TCT** Television Network

youtube.com/CappsMinistries
facebook.com/CharlesCappsMinistries

BOOKS BY CHARLES CAPPS
AND ANNETTE CAPPS

Angels

God's Creative Power® for Finances

God's Creative Power® - Gift Edition
(Also available in Spanish)

BOOKS BY ANNETTE CAPPS

Quantum Faith®

Reverse The Curse in
Your Body and Emotions

Removing the Roadblocks to Health and Healing

Overcoming Persecution

BOOKS BY CHARLES CAPPS

NEW RELEASE!-Calling Things That Are Not

Triumph Over The Enemy

When Jesus Prays Through You

The Tongue – A Creative Force

Releasing the Ability of God Through Prayer

End Time Events

Your Spiritual Authority

Changing the Seen and Shaping The Unseen

Faith That Will Not Change

Faith and Confession

God's Creative Power® Will Work For You
(Also available in Spanish)

God's Creative Power® For Healing
(Also available in Spanish)

Success Motivation Through the Word

God's Image of You

Seedtime and Harvest
(Also available in Spanish)

The Thermostat of Hope
(Also available in Spanish under the title
Hope- A Partner to Faith)

How You Can Avoid Tragedy

Kicking Over Sacred Cows

The Substance of Things

The Light of Life in the Spirit of Man

Faith That Will Work For You

Charles Capps a farmer from England, Arkansas became an internationally known Bible teacher by sharing practical truths from the Word of God. His simplistic, down to earth  style of applying spiritual principles to daily life has appealed to people from every Christian denomination.

The requests for speaking engagements became so great after the printing of *God's Creative Power® Will Work for You* that he retired from farming and became a full-time Bible teacher. His books are available in multiple languages throughout the world.

Besides publishing 24 books, including best-sellers *The Tongue A Creative Force* and *God's Creative Power®* series which has sold over 6 million copies, Capps Ministries has a national daily radio broadcast and weekly TV broadcast called "Concepts of Faith".